Instant Bible Lessons for toddlers

Jesus Teaches Me

Mary J. Davis

These pages may be copied.
Permission is granted to the buyer of this book to
photocopy student materials for use with
Sunday school or Bible teaching classes.

For information regarding the CPSIA on printed material call:
203-595-3636 and provide reference # LANC-538867

rainbowpublishers®

Rainbow Publishers • P.O. Box 261129 • San Diego, CA 92196
www.RainbowPublishers.com

Dedication

What a privilege to develop ideas for teachers or parents to use to teach their toddlers about God! I dedicate this book to you.

Also, to Larry, to our children and grandchildren.

Instant Bible Lessons for Toddlers: Jesus Teaches Me
©2014 by Rainbow Publishers, second printing
ISBN 10: 1-58411-124-0
ISBN 13: 978-1-58411-124-5
Rainbow reorder# RB38216
RELIGION / Christian Ministry / Children

Rainbow Publishers
P.O. Box 261129
San Diego, CA 92196
www.RainbowPublishers.com

Cover Illustrator: Stacey Lamb
Interior Illustrator: Darren McKee

Printed in the United States of America

■ ■ ■ Contents ■ ■ ■

▪●▪ Introduction ▪●▪

Do your toddlers know what Jesus teaches in the Bible? Knowing that Jesus teaches us important values and truths is a first step in growing in the Lord. After they participate in the activities in *Jesus Teaches Me*, toddlers will begin to implement important values in their everyday lives. Letting our lights shine, growing strong in the Lord, obeying the Word, forgiving, being good for God, praying, and living as children of God are values even toddlers can learn.

Each of the first eight chapters includes a Bible story, memory verse, and a variety of activities to help reinforce the truth in the lesson. An additional chapter contains miscellaneous projects that can be used anytime throughout the study or at the end to review the lessons.

The most exciting aspect of *Instant Bible Lessons for Toddlers*, which includes *My Amazing God*, *Jesus Teaches Me*, *I Can Help God*, and *I Believe in Jesus*, is its flexibility. You can easily adapt these lessons to a Sunday school hour, a children's church service, a Wednesday night Bible study or family home use. And, because there is a variety of reproducible ideas from which to choose (see below), you will enjoy creating a learning session that is best for your group of students, whether large or small, beginning or advanced, active or studious. The intriguing topics will keep your kids coming back for more, week after week.

With these lessons, toddlers will learn the values that Jesus teaches them.

✳ How to Use This Book ✳

Each chapter begins with a Bible story which you may read to your class in one of two levels, followed by discussion questions. Following each story page is a story visual for you to make and use as you tell the story. Every story chapter also includes a bulletin board poster with the memory verse and suggestions for using the poster as an activity. All the activities are tagged with one of the icons below, so you can quickly flip through the chapter and select the projects you need. Simply cut off the teacher instructions on the pages and duplicate!

story to share   story visual   bulletin board   simple craft   activity

easy puzzle   coloring   song/verse   game   snack

Chapter 1

Letting Our Light Shine for Jesus

Memory Verse

Let your light shine.
— *Matthew 5:16*

Story to Share

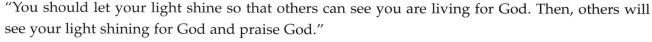

2's and 3's ↝

Many people gathered to hear Jesus teach them. It was wonderful to hear Jesus talk about God and heaven, and about how we can live for him.

"You can be a light in the world," Jesus said. "You should let your light shine so that others can see you are living for God. Then, others will see your light shining for God and praise God."

Jesus taught about shining lights. "Don't light a lamp, then hide it under a bowl or in a basket. When you light a lamp, put it on a stand so that everyone in the house can see it."

We don't turn on our lights at home, then cover them up so that it is very dark. We let the light shine and light up our whole house.

Jesus says we are like a light. We should shine so that everyone can see.

1's and young 2's ↝

People loved to hear Jesus teach them.

"You are the light of the world," Jesus said. "When you light a lamp at home, you don't hide it under a bowl. You let it shine in the house so that everyone can see."

"Let your light shine for God," Jesus told the people. "Then others will see your light and praise God."

Based on Matthew 5:14-16

Questions for Discussion

1. What does Jesus say we are? A light in the world.

2. What should we NOT do with our lights? Hide them.

story visual

What You Need

- duplicated page (on white paper)
- black construction paper
- flashlight

What to Do

1. Cut out the flashlight slip-cover. Fit the cover around your flashlight, and tape the seams. Do the same with black construction paper.

2. To tell the story, hold the flashlight. Tell about our lights shining for God. Slip the white slip-cover over the flashlight, then turn the flashlight on. When the story says, "do not hide your lamp under a bowl," turn the flashlight off and slip the black slip-cover over the flashlight. Let children hold or touch the flashlight. Say, **The light isn't shining. Jesus tells us not to cover up our light. We are a light in the world.**

• Flashlight Slip-covers •

LET YOUR LIGHT SHINE.
~Matthew 5:16

Another Idea

Shine the flashlight on each child, (not in their eyes) one at a time. Say each child's name, "Claire is letting her light shine for Jesus. Now Jason is letting his light shine for Jesus."

• Bulletin Board Poster •

Poster Pointer

Make a coloring house: Use an up-side-down box, about waist-high to children. Each week, tape several of that week's story posters to the sides and flat surface of the box. Provide crayons. Supervise several children coloring at the "coloring house" together. Talk about the story as the children work on the pictures.

What You Need
- pattern on page 10
- construction paper or card stock
- black construction paper
- tape

What to Do
1. Depending on how you want to use the poster (see ideas below), enlarge, reduce, or simply copy page 10 to fit your bulletin board space.
2. To use the poster as an in-class activity, cut a 3-inch square of black paper for each child. Help the children place the square flap over the light in the picture. Place a piece of tape along the top of the black square. Show the children how to lift the flap to "let your light shine," then put the flap down to "hide your light."

• Light Shine •

• Shining Light Song •

Shining Light

Twinkle, twinkle, shining light.

[wiggle fingers, to indicate twinkling lights]

God wants my light to shine bright.

[point to self, then place hands at each side of face with fingers spread open]

Others will see my light and praise God

    [point to God]

    That's what it says, in God's Word.

    [make a book with hands, palms up, little finger-sides together]

    Twinkle, twinkle, shining light.

    [open and close hands several times to indicate twinkling lights]

    God wants my light to shine bright.

[point to self, then place hands at each side of face with fingers spread open]

My Light, Your Light!

My light shines for God. *[point to self]*

Your light shines for God. *[point to others]*

God is pleased when we let our lights shine. *[point to God]*

Our lights shine for God. *[point to self and then others]*

---

song/verse

What You Need
- duplicated page

What to Do

1. Before class, practice singing, "Shining Light" and learn the actions to show the children.

2. Sing the song "Shining Light," to the tune of "Twinkle, Twinkle". Encourage the children to do the actions as they sing the song with you.

3. Say the action verse, "My Light, Your Light" with the children. Encourage children to do the actions with you while saying the easy verse.

•Light Shine•

simple craft

What You Need

- duplicated page for each child
- pint jar for each child.
- scissors
- tape
- chenille stems
- small glow sticks

What to Do

1. Before class, cut out a lantern top circle from the pattern page for each child. Cut on the solid line. Overlap the cut edges to form a cone-style top for each lantern.

2. Help older toddlers place an end of two chenille stems into the rim of the jar with the lid off.

3. Place a glow stick inside each jar. Place lid on the jar tightly and tie the stems into a handle.

4. Attach the cone-style paper lantern top over lid with pieces of tape.

5. Say, **Jesus wants us to let our lights shine for God.**

•Light Shine•

• Lantern •

Let your light shine.
~ Matthew 5:15

• Making Light Puzzle •

What You Need
- duplicated page for each child
- crayons

What to Do
1. Give each child a puzzle page.
2. For the puzzle at the top of the page, help the children use a crayon to make a mark on the items that make light.
3. When the children have finished the puzzle, have them color the children at the bottom of the page. Say, **Jesus wants us to let our lights shine for God.**

•Light Shine•

coloring

What You Need
- duplicated page for each child
- crayons

What to Do
1. Give each child a copy of the page to color.
2. Read the story to the children as they color the pictures.

• Light in the Darkness •

"Grandpa's here!" Tracy opened the door and jumped into Grandpa's arms.

"What are we going to do while you baby-sit for me tonight?" Tracy knew that Grandpa always had a fun plan. What fun it was when Grandpa came to baby-sit.

"We are going to take a walk outdoors in the dark," Grandpa said.

"Oh, I don't like it out in the dark," Tracy told Grandpa.

"But, I have a special surprise," Grandpa said.

After Mom and Dad left, Tracy asked Grandpa, "Are we really going to take a walk outdoors in the dark?"

Grandpa gave Tracy a bag. She looked inside. "It's a flashlight!"

Tracy and Grandpa walked outdoors for a long time. Sometimes, Tracy turned the flashlight off to see how dark it was. Then, she turned the flashlight right back on.

"I still don't like the dark," she said.

Grandpa said, "Jesus wants us to be like a light in the darkness. We can do good things for God and people will see our good deeds. People will praise God that we are a light in the world."

Tracy shined the flashlight on herself. "I am a light in the world."

Grandpa and Tracy laughed while they walked home.

• Lights of Kindness •

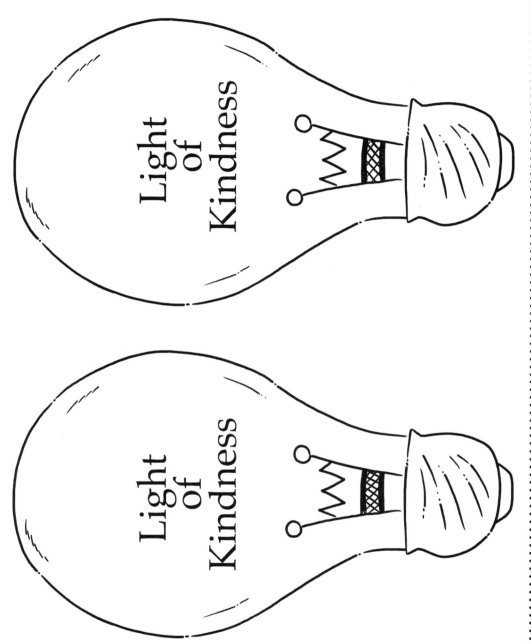

Light of Kindness

Light of Kindness

activity

What You Need
- page duplicated to yellow paper
- tape

What to Do

1. Before class, cut out several of the light bulbs, at least 2 or 3 for each student.

2. Say, **We are going to be "lights of kindness" today. Each time you do something kind, you can have a light to wear on your clothes.**

3. Encourage the children to help each other, share toys, say kind words. Use loops of tape to fasten a light to each child as he/she is doing kind things.

4. Say, **Remember that Jesus teaches us to be a light in the world. Others will see our good deeds and praise God.**

• Light Shine •

• Light of the World Game •

game

What You Need
- page duplicated to yellow paper
- black construction paper
- scissors
- tape
- beanbags

What to Do

1. Before class, duplicate 10 or more yellow verse circles. Cut out the yellow circles. Cut out 5 or more black circles from construction paper.

2. Tape the circles to the floor in a large group.

3. Have the children take turns tossing a beanbag onto the grouping of circles. When a child's beanbag lands on a yellow circle, say, **Lyn's light is shining.** When a child's beanbag lands on a black circle, let the child try again.

Let your light shine.
~ Matthew 5:15

Let your light shine.
~ Matthew 5:15

Chapter 2

Growing Strong Because We Heard God's Word

Memory Verse

Hear the Word [of God].
– *Mark 4:20*

Story to Share

2's and 3's

Jesus told a story to many people: "A farmer scattered seeds so they would grow. Some seeds fell along the path, and birds came and ate it all up. Some seeds fell on rocky ground. The hot sun burned up the plants. Some seeds grew, but thorns and weeds grew up around the plants. Some seeds fell on good ground. Those plants grew up big and strong."

Jesus told his helpers, "The seeds in the story are the Word of God. Sometimes people hear the Word and don't grow in the Lord. But, others hear the Word and use it to serve God."

I's and young 2's ⤳

Jesus told this story: "A farmer put some seeds on the ground to grow. Birds came along and ate some of the seeds. The sun was very hot and some of the seeds could not grow into plants. Weeds grew around some of the plants and the plants could not grow any more. But, other seeds landed on good places and the seeds grew into big, strong plants."

"The seeds are like God's Word," Jesus said. "Some people hear the Word of God and it does not help them. Others hear the Word of God and obey God."

Based on Mark 4:2-20

Questions for Discussion

1. What ate up some of the seeds? Birds.

2. What did Jesus say the seeds are? The Word of God.

story visual

What You Need
- duplicated page
- craft sticks
- tape
- Styrofoam, about 8 x 10 inches

What to Do

1. Before class, cut out the story figures. Tape each figure to a craft stick.

2. To tell the story, press the craft stick end into the foam to stand up. Keep the farmer in the scene all the time. Add the figures as you tell the story.

Another Idea

Bring some fresh food items, a plant, and some seeds to class. Show each of the items and a matching story figure. Discuss how the seeds are put into soil, then grow into plants.

Then show a Bible. Say, **Hear the Word of God so you may grow up big and strong, just like the plants the farmer grew.**

• Stand-up Story •

• Bulletin Board Poster •

bulletin board

What You Need
• pattern on page 20
• construction paper or card stock
• glue
• bird seed

What to Do
1. Depending on how you want to use the poster (see ideas below), enlarge, reduce, or simply copy page 20 to fit your bulletin board space.
2. To use the poster as an in-class activity, spread some glue on the ground part in each picture of the poster. Let children sprinkle some seeds in the glue.

Poster Pointer

Place a box on a special table each week. Inside the box, have several copies of the poster, and one or more of the items on the following list. Change the items around each week so children have something different to do each class session.

• Colored chalks
• Cotton swabs and water colors
• Sticker dots to outline the posters
• Cereal pieces to fill in the picture
• Glue and yarn lengths to outline pictures or frame the poster
• Colored sugars and glue.

Spread glue on parts of the poster, and sprinkle on colored sugars for a sand-like painting. Punch holes along the edge of posters and provide lengths of yarn for toddlers to lace through holes in the poster.

• Seed Sower •

19

• Double Gift Card •

GOD'S WORD FALLS ON OUR EARS TO HELP US GROW STRONG INTO THE LORD.

Bible +

SEEDS THAT FELL ON GOOD SOIL GREW INTO STRONG PLANTS.

simple craft

. . . .

What You Need
- duplicated page for each child
- crayons
- packet of seeds for each child
- very small Bible for each child (can substitute Bible stickers)
- tape

What to Do
1. Before class, cut the card from the page for each student.
2. Have students color both sides of the card.
3. Inside the 'seed' side of the card, tape a packet of seeds.
4. Inside the 'God's Word' side of the card, tape a small Bible or have students stick on a Bible sticker.
5. Say, **You can give a special gift to someone. We are giving our special friends a packet of seeds to grow. And, we're giving them a Bible so they may HEAR GOD'S WORD.**

• Seed Sower •

song

. . . .

What You Need
• duplicated page

What to Do
1. Practice singing the song, "Hear God's Word" to the tune of "Skip To My Lou."
2. Sing the song with the children.
3. Add a simple action to the song by touching your ears when you say the word, HEAR.
4. Practice singing the song, "A Farmer Scattered Seed," to the tune of "Farmer in the Dell."
5. Sing the song with the children. You may add simple actions by pretending to scatter seeds, then cupping a hand around your ear to "hear God's Word."

• Seed Sower •

• God's Word Songs •

Hear God's Word

Hear, hear, hear, God's Word
Hear, hear, hear God's Word
Hear, hear, hear God's Word
Hear God's Word and grow strong.

A Farmer Scattered Seed

A farmer scattered seeds
A farmer scattered seeds
Some seeds grew strong and some did not.
A farmer scattered seeds.

We should hear God's Word
We should hear God's Word
Then we will grow strong and good
We should hear God's Word.

• Hear and Grow Game •

HEAR GOD'S
WORD AND GROW!

game

What You Need
- duplicated page
- scissors
- tape
- small paper or plastic plate

What to Do
1. Cut the circle from the page. Glue the circle to the inside center of the paper plate to make a flying disc.
2. To play the game, arrange the children in a circle. Stand in the center. Tell the children to crouch down like a little seed. (Show them how to crouch down, if very young toddlers.)
3. Scoot the plate along the floor to one of the children. Say, **Lexie can hear God's Word and grow.** Show the children how to 'spring up tall' when they catch the 'Word' disc.
4. Continue the game until each child has caught the flying disc.

• Seed Sower •

coloring

What You Need
- duplicated page for each child
- crayons

What to Do
1. Hold the picture up so that all the children can see it while you read the story out loud to the children.
2. Afterward, while the children color their pictures, ask, **What book do we read to find out God's Word?**

• I Hear God's Word •

Jeremy was all dressed and ready to go to Sunday school. "I love to go to my class," he told Mommy and Daddy.

Daddy smiled. "I like to go to Sunday school and hear God's Word, too," he said.

Everyone was ready to go out the door.

"Wait!" Jeremy ran to his room. Soon, he came back to the hallway. "I almost forgot my Bible," he said.

Jeremy carried his Bible out to the car. He held it very tightly until he got to Sunday school.

"Hello, Jeremy," Mrs. Anderson said when Jeremy came into the classroom. "I see you remembered to bring your Bible."

Jeremy smiled. He was proud that he remembered to bring his Bible.

"Let's read a story from Jeremy's Bible," Mrs. Anderson said.

Jeremy gave his Bible to the teacher. All the other kids sat down on the story rug. Mrs. Anderson read a story about a farmer who scattered seeds on the ground to grow. Some seeds were eaten by birds. Some seeds were burned by the sun. Some seeds were choked by big thorns and weeds. But, some seeds grew big and strong.

"The big, strong plants that grew are just like us," Mrs. Anderson said. "When we hear God's Word, we can grow strong in the Lord."

Jeremy liked that story. He was glad he had a Bible so that he could hear God's Word and grow big and strong in the Lord.

• From a Small Seed •

easy puzzle

What You Need
- duplicated page for each child
- crayons

What to Do
1. Give each child a puzzle page.
2. Have children trace the apple with red crayon and color the seeds. Say, **The apple seed grows into a tree that gives us yummy apples.**
3. Have children trace the pumpkin with an orange crayon and color the seeds. Say, **The pumpkin seed grows into a big orange pumpkin.**
4. Have children touch the picture of the Bible. Say, **When we hear the Word of God, we can grow big and strong. Our memory verse says, "Hear the Word of God."** Help the children finish drawing the picture of the child by tracing the dashed lines.

• Seed Sower •

simple craft

What You Need
- duplicated page for each child
- 2 paper cups for each child
- scissors
- tape or glue

What to Do

1. Before class, cut the ears from the pattern page for each child. Cut the bottoms from two paper cups for each child. Tape or glue one ear onto each cup, with the 'hearing' part of the ears facing the largest end of the cups.

2. Give each child a set of the 'ears.'

3. Show the children how to hold the ears up to their own ears to 'hear.' Retell the story or sing some familiar songs with the children.

4. Say, **We use our ears to hear God's Word so we can grow big and strong for the Lord.**

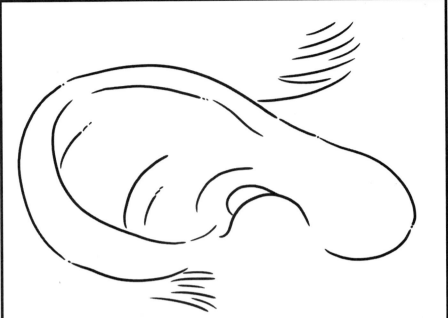

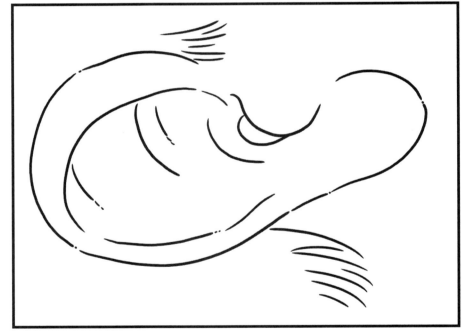

■● Chapter 3 ●■
The Wise and Foolish Builder

Memory Verse

If you love me, you will obey.
— *John 14:15*

Story to Share

2's and 3's ～→

Jesus asked why some of his followers would not obey him. Jesus told a story to show how important it is that we obey him.

A wise man built a house on solid rock. A storm and flood came. Water and strong wind hit against the house. But, the house did not shake or fall.

A foolish man built his house on the sand. A storm and flood came. The house could not stand up against the wind and rain. The house CRASHED.

Jesus wanted us to learn that we should obey him. When we build our life on Jesus, we will obey. We will be able to stand strong.

If we do not obey Jesus, we will be like the house that crashed in the storm.

I's and young 2's ～→

A wise man built his house on a rock. A storm came. Rain hit against the house. Wind blew against the house. But the house did not fall down.

A foolish man built his house on the sand. A storm came. Rain hit against the house. Wind blew against the house. The house went CRASH and fell down.

Jesus says, if we obey him, we will be strong like the house the wise man built.

Based on Luke 6:46-49

Questions for Discussion

I. If we obey Jesus, which man are we like? The wise man.

2. What happened to the house of the man who built his house on the sand? It CRASHED!

story visual

What You Need
- page duplicated to paper, two copies
- soup-sized can
- toilet tissue tube
- scissors
- tape

What to Do

1. Before class, cut out the two houses from the pattern page. Tape one house to the soup can and one to the tissue tube.

2. To tell the story, stand the soup can on the table. Tell the story of the wise man. Have children try to blow the house down.

3. Then, place the tissue tube on the table. Tell the story of the foolish man. Have children blow on the house to make it fall over.

4. Say, **When we obey Jesus, we are like the strong house that the wise man built. Jesus wants us to be strong for him.**

• **Builders** •

• Two Houses •

Another Idea

Put some rocks in a plastic sandwich-sized bag. Put some sand (or yellow corn meal) in another bag. Seal the bags securely with tape. Let the children touch the hard rocks and the soft sand. Say, **The wise man built his house on the rocks so it wouldn't fall down in a storm. Can you feel how hard the rocks are? The foolish man built his house on the sand, and it went CRASH in a storm. Can you feel how soft the sand is? Jesus wants us to obey him so we will be like the strong house on the rock.**

• Bulletin Board Poster •

Poster Pointer

Poster Garland: Hang a length of crepe paper streamer along a wall, at eye level for toddlers. Tape each week's poster to the crepe paper to form a garland. Or let the children glue crepe paper around the poster to form a frame.

bulletin board

What You Need
- page 30 duplicated for each child
- glue
- tape
- 1 pint milk cartons
- crayons

What to Do
1. Copy page 30 to fit your bulletin board.
2. To use the poster as an in-class activity, copy page 30 for each child. Write, "The wise man built his house on a rock" along the bottom of the page.
3. Let children color the pictures using crayons while you tell the story on page 27.
4. Help children wrap the house pictures around the milk cartons and tape them.
5. Say the memory verse with the children.

•Builders•

• Obey Game •

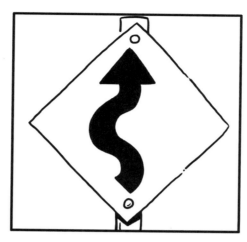

game

What You Need
- duplicated page
- markers or crayon
- scissors
- glue
- tape
- Optional – CD player and Sunday school favorite songs CD

What to Do
1. Before class, cut out several of each picture square.
2. Color the stop sign red, the stop light green, and the two direction signs yellow.
3. Glue each picture square to a separate piece of construction paper. Glue a Bible below each sign.
4. Tape the signs to the wall, around the room.
5. Lead children in a walk. Stop at each sign. Say, **When we travel, we need to obey signs to stay safe. Jesus wants us to obey God's Word, the Bible.**

•Builders•

song/verse

What You Need
• duplicated page

What to Do

1. Practice singing, "Be Wise and Obey," to the tune of "Pop Goes the Weasel."

2. Sing the song with the children. Do the action listed after each line with a **BOLD** printed word.

3. Say the action verse, showing children the actions. Repeat the verse, encouraging the children to say the verse and do the actions with you.

• Be Wise and Obey Song •

Be Wise and Obey Song

The foolish man built his house on sand
The winds and rain came all around.
The house couldn't stand up in the storm
CRASH the house fell down! *[clap hands together loudly]*

The wise man built his house on rock
The winds and rain came all around.
The house stood strong in the storm.
HOORAY, the house wouldn't fall down! *[wave hands in air]*

I will be wise and obey God's Word
Troubles can come all around.
I will obey and be strong.
NOTHING can make me fall down! *[shake head "no" vigorously]*

Luke 6:46-49

I am Strong – Action Verse

I am strong like the house on the rock *[flex muscles]*
Not weak like the house on the sand.
I am wise and obey God's Word. *[point up]*
This makes me very strong for my Lord. *[flex muscles]*

• Wise Builder Storm Globe •

simple craft

. . . .

What You Need
- duplicated page for each child
- small, clear plastic jar with lid
- tape
- blue glitter or sequins
- scissors

What to Do
1. Cut out the two house pictures from this page for each child.
2. Tape pictures to the inside of the jar with the images facing outward.
3. Let each child help sprinkle some blue glitter or sequins in the jar.
4. Place the lid on the jar securely.
5. Show children how to shake the jar and see the "storm" moving. Say, **The wind and rain won't make the house fall because the wise man built it on a rock. We won't fall because we obey God's Word.**

Luke 6:46-49   Luke 6:46-49

•Builders•

33

coloring

What You Need
- duplicated page for each child
- crayons

What to Do
1. Hold the picture up so that all the children can see it while you read the story out loud to the children.
2. Afterward, while the children color their pictures, say, **Can you tell about a time when you didn't obey?**

• When You Don't Obey •

Christopher put his favorite cars in a row on the floor. "Zoom," he said. "I like the orange race car the best." He put the orange car under Mom's rocking chair. "This can be my garage."

"Don't put your cars under the rocking chair," Mom said. "If you forget to pick one up, it can be broken when someone sits in the chair."

Christopher didn't pick up his car.

After supper, Daddy, Mommy, and Christopher went to the living room. Daddy sat down in the rocking chair.

CRUNCH!

"My orange car!" Christopher looked at his broken car. "My favorite car is smashed."

Mommy put the car in Christopher's hand. "You didn't obey me when I asked you to keep your cars away from the rocker."

Christopher began to cry.

Daddy put his arms around Christopher. "Do you remember when we read the Bible story last night about the wise and foolish builders? What happened to the foolish man who built his house on the sand?"

"His house crashed in the storm," Christopher said. "My car crashed under the rocker."

"'Jesus told the story of the wise and foolish builders to help us remember to obey God. When you didn't obey Mommy, you weren't obeying God."

"I'm sorry I didn't obey," Christopher said. He took his favorite car to his room and put it on his dresser. "I want to remember to obey."

• Hidden Picture Puzzle •

easy puzzle

What You Need
- duplicated page for each child
- crayons

What to Do
1. Give each child a puzzle page.
2. Say, **The wise man built his house on a rock. The storm couldn't knock the house down. Jesus told this story to teach us that we will be strong in the Lord if we obey God's Word.**
3. Help the children find and color the following hidden items: Two lightning bolts, two raindrops, two umbrellas, two rain boots, two raincoats.
4. Say, **These are things we might find when it is raining. Rain will remind us of Jesus' story of the wise and foolish builders. We can remember to obey God's Word.**

•Builders•

activity

What You Need
- duplicated page
- optional –
  cardboard, glue

What to Do

1. Place the story page on a table, or hold it so that all children can see it.

2. Have older toddlers tell you the story. Encourage each child along these lines:

**Mommy put some yummy cookies on the table. She told the little boy not to get into the cookies yet.
The little boy got on his tiptoes to reach the cookies. But, the little boy knew he should obey Mommy.
"You obeyed me," Mommy said. "You may have the first cookie."
Jesus said, "If you love me, you will obey."**

• No-Read Story •

Option

You might want to glue the picture onto cardboard so it is easy for children to handle.

■● Chapter 4 ●■
We Learn to Forgive Others

Memory Verse

Forgive ... from your heart.
— *Matthew 18:35*

✱Story to Share✱

2's and 3's ⟿

Peter asked Jesus, "How many times should I forgive my brother? Up to seven times?"

Jesus said, "Not seven times, but seventy-seven."

Jesus told a story about a servant who owed his king a lot of money. The servant begged the king not to put him in jail. The king said, "I forgive you."

The servant went out to find someone who owed him money. "I am going to put you in jail if you don't pay me back right now," the servant said. The man begged for forgiveness, but the servant would not forgive and had him put into jail. The king heard what this servant had done and he put the servant into jail.

Jesus said, "This is how my heavenly Father will treat each of you unless you forgive your brother from your heart."

I's and young 2's ⟿

Jesus told a story about forgiving others: A servant owed his king a lot of money. The king was going to put the servant in jail. "Please forgive me," the servant begged. The king forgave him.

But the man found someone who owed him money and had him put in jail. The king heard this and put the servant in jail. Jesus said, "Forgive your brother from your heart."

Based on Matthew 18:23-35

Questions for Discussion

1. What did the king do to the servant who owed him a lot? Forgave him.

2. What does Jesus want us to do to others? Forgive others.

story visual

What You Need
• duplicated page
• card stock
• scissors
• glue

What to Do
1. Cut the four scenes from the page. Enlarge each story scene. Glue each scene to a piece of card stock.
2. To tell the story, hold each story card so the children can see it. Change the scenes as you progress with telling the story.

More Ideas
Duplicate the pattern page for each child to take home. Bring the concept of forgiveness to life for the children by watching for situations in which a child is upset or someone doesn't want to share a toy. Say, **Jesus wants us to forgive from our heart. Let's hug each other and forgive.**

• Forgive •

• Forgive from Your Heart • Story Cards

• Bulletin Board Poster •

What You Need
- pattern on page 40
- construction paper or card stock
- heart stickers

What to Do

1. Depending on how you want to use the poster (see ideas below), enlarge, reduce, or simply copy page 40 to fit your bulletin board space.

2. To use the poster as an in-class activity, have the children outline the poster with heart stickers.

3. Recite the story and say the memory verse with the children.

Poster Pointer

Parent information: Fasten a letter-sized file box onto the wall outside your classroom, or set a file box on a table just outside your door. Duplicate a poster for each child every week with a few extras in case of visitors. Duplicate news, announcements, or the Bible story onto the back of the poster. Place a sign close to the box of posters, inviting parents to take one home.

• Forgive •

Forgive...from your heart. ~Matthew 18:35

• I Will Forgive •

"When Someone breaks my toy."		" I WILL FORGIVE"
"When someone hits or hurts me."		" I WILL FORGIVE"
"When someone doesn't share with me."		" I WILL FORGIVE"

activity

What You Need
- duplicated page for each child
- scissors
- tape
- string or yarn

What to Do

1. Before class, cut the 9 rectangles from the pattern page.

2. Cut three 5-inch lengths of string. Tape one end of a string to the center of a picture rectangle. Tape a heart onto the other end of the string.

3. Read each of the situations, one at a time. Say, **When someone breaks your toy, what does Jesus want you to do? Jesus wants you to forgive from your heart. Let's place the heart on the picture.** (Repeat for each one of the pictures.)

• Forgive •

song

. . . .

What You Need
• duplicated page

What to Do

1. Before class, practice singing "The Forgiving Song."

2. Sing the song to the tune of "Wheels on the Bus." Sing as many verses as you wish. Older children will enjoy singing all the verses with you.

• The Forgiving Song •

Jesus Said, STOP!

When someone makes me angry, I'll forgive
I'll forgive
I'll forgive
When someone makes me angry, I'll forgive
Jesus says to forgive.

When a friend won't share with me, I'll forgive
I'll forgive
I'll forgive
When a friend won't share with me, I'll forgive
Jesus says to forgive.

When my sister breaks my doll, I'll forgive
I'll forgive
I'll forgive
When my sister breaks my doll, I'll forgive
Jesus says to forgive.

When my brother takes my toy, I'll forgive
I'll forgive
I'll forgive
When my brother takes my toy, I'll forgive
Jesus says to forgive.

Jesus teaches me to forgive
To forgive
To forgive
Jesus teaches me to forgive
Jesus says to forgive.

• Forgiving Makes Me Happy •

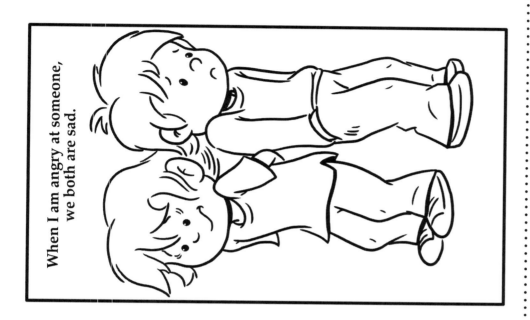

When I am angry at someone, we both are sad.

But, when I forgive, that makes us both glad.

simple craft

What You Need
- page for each child
- card-sized envelopes, at least 3 x 5 inches
- scissors
- crayons
- glue

What to Do
1. Cut the two children shapes from the page.
2. Seal the envelope closed. Cut open one narrow end of the envelope.
3. Help children glue one child shape to the front and one child shape onto the back of the envelope, with the bottom end of the pictures toward the cut-open end of the envelope.
4. Slip the envelope over child's hand. Read each side of the craft to the children. Show children how to flip from the sad children to the happy children.

•Forgive•

What You Need
- duplicated page for each child
- crayons

What to Do
1. Hold the picture up so that all the children can see it while you read the story out loud to the children.
2. Afterward, while the children color their pictures, say, **Can you tell about a time when you had to forgive someone?**

• A Brother Forgives •

"Catch the ball!" Bryce yelled at Joel.

Joel looked up just in time to see the ball hit Mom's favorite lamp. CRASH!

"Mom said we can't play ball in the house," Joel said.

Bryce ran into the other room. "Mom," he yelled. "Joel broke your lamp."

Mom came running into the living room. "Oh, Joel," she said.

"Are you going to tell me you are sorry?" Mom asked.

Joel whispered a quick, "Sorry." Then, he ran to his bedroom.

Later, Mom called the boys down to dinner.

"I'm not hungry," Joel yelled downstairs. "I'm angry at Bryce and I'm not going to eat dinner with him!"

Soon, Mom and Bryce came upstairs. "Bryce told me that he was the one who broke the lamp," Mom said. "Bryce is sorry."

"Yeah," Bryce said. "I am sorry. Will you forgive me?"

"I am angry," Joel said. "I had to tell you I was sorry for something I didn't do."

Mom said, "Remember that Jesus taught us in the story of the servant who was forgiven by the king, then the servant wouldn't forgive his own friend?"

Joel remembered the story. He knew Jesus wanted him to forgive Bryce. "Okay," he said. "I forgive you, Bryce. I'm not angry anymore."

"Thanks," Bryce said.

• Forgive •

• Happy to Forgive •

Jesus Said, STOP!

I am happy when I forgive my friends. *[Clap clap]*
I am happy when I forgive my friends. *[Clap clap]*
I am happy when I forgive others and they forgive me.
I am happy when I forgive my friends. *[Clap clap]*

I am happy when my friends forgive me. *[Clap clap]*
I am happy when my friends forgive me. *[Clap clap]*
I am happy when I forgive others, and they forgive me.
I am happy when my friends forgive me. *[Clap clap]*

What You Need
• duplicated page

What to Do
1. Sing the song "Happy to Forgive" to the tune of "If You're Happy and You Know It" with the children.
2. Encourage the children to sing the song with you, clapping when you clap.

• Forgiving Game •

game

What You Need

- duplicated page (duplicate page to brightly colored paper for a colorful baton)
- paper towel tube
- glue

What to Do

1. Before class, wrap the duplicated page around the paper towel tube to make a baton.

2. To play the game, arrange the children in a circle. Pass the baton to one child and have him/her pass it back to you. Repeat with each child. Go faster and faster. DROP the baton now and then. Say, **Oh, I dropped the baton, Chris. Will you forgive me?**

3. Say the memory verse with the children after the game is finished.

Forgive... from Your Heart.
~ Matthew 18:35

•Forgive•

•■ Chapter 5 •■

Jesus Teaches Me to be Good

Memory Verse

Let's not become weary in doing good.
– Galatians 6:9

Story to Share

2's and 3's ⤳

Jesus told a story to teach us what heaven will be like.

Jesus said, "A net was put down into the water and caught all kinds of fish. When the net was full, the fishermen pulled it up onto the shore. The fishermen sat down to separate the fish. They put good fish into a basket so the fishermen and their families could eat the good fish. They threw the bad fish away."

Jesus says heaven will be like the fishing net. Angels will separate the good people from the bad. Good people are those who trust and obey God.

1's and young 2's ⤳

Jesus told a story about catching fish. Fishermen caught lots of fish in their nets. The fishermen put the good fish in a basket and they threw the bad fish away. In heaven, good people will get to stay with God. Jesus wants us to be good.

Based on Matthew 13:47-50

Questions for Discussion

1. What did the fishermen do with the good and bad fish? They put the good fish in baskets and threw the bad fish away.

2. Who will get to stay in heaven with God? People who trust and obey God.

story visual

What You Need

- duplicated page, 2 or more copies
- basket
- trash can, small
- scissors
- story poster, page 50

What to Do

1. Cut out several fish.
2. To tell the story, have children hold some fish. Have them put some fish in the basket and some in the trash can.
3. Tell about the fishermen catching a net full of fish, and separating the good fish from the bad.
4. Show the story poster to the children.

• Good and Bad Fish •

More Ideas

Cut some fish from the pattern page. Let each child glue at least one fish onto a piece of poster board. Glue or staple a piece of produce netting onto the poster board. Have the children sit on a blanket for a net. Touch each child and say, "You are a good fish. You do good things for God."

• Fish •

• Bulletin Board Poster •

Poster Pointer

Sturdy book: Reduce the size of each of the eight story posters in this book, copying each poster to a brightly colored sheet of paper. Also, reduce and copy page 89, from chapter 9, for the book cover. Cover both sides of each reduced-size poster and the book cover with clear self-stick plastic. Use clear, heavy tape to form a binding on the outside of the book, as well as along the seams of each page in the book. Let children hold the books as you review the lessons or memory verses.

bulletin board

What You Need
- pattern on page 50
- construction paper or card stock
- string or yarn
- jumbo craft sticks
- glue
- crayons

What to Do
1. Depending on how you want to use the poster (see ideas below), enlarge, reduce, or simply copy page 50 to fit your bulletin board space.

2. To use the poster as an in-class activity, glue the story posters onto construction paper for sturdiness. Give each child six jumbo craft sticks. Have the children color the craft sticks with crayon. Help the children glue craft sticks around the edge to form a frame for the poster picture. Tape a loop of string or yarn to form a hanger.

• Fish •

• Good Things Puzzle •

easy puzzle

What You Need
- duplicated page for each child
- crayons

What to Do
1. Give each child a puzzle page.
2. Tell children to put a mark on each thing that is good. Discuss each picture:
**The boy and girl are praying to God. Is it good to pray to God? Yes, it is good to pray to God.
What is this building? Yes, it's a church. Is it good to go to church? Of course.
What is this book? Yes, It's a Bible. Is it good to learn the Bible? Yes, it is very good.
What is the Mommy giving the little boy and girl in this picture? A hug! Is a hug a good thing to get? Yes, it is good to get a hug from mommy or daddy.**

•Fish•

simple craft

What You Need
- duplicated page
- ½ gallon plastic milk jugs
- crepe paper streamers, three 2-foot lengths for each child
- scissors and tape

What to Do

1. Cut top off of milk jugs just below the handle. Cut the fish and the story theme picture strip from the page.

2. Help children tape one fish to one end of each of the three lengths of crepe paper streamers. Tie the opposite end of each streamer to the handle of the milk jug 'net.'

3. Tape the story theme strip onto the milk jug.

4. Say, **Jesus taught about catching fish. The good fish are put into baskets and the bad fish are thrown away. Jesus teaches us to be good.**

• **Fish** •

• Fill the Net •

• Good Fish Song •

Some Good Fish

This is the way we catch some fish
[pretend to pull in nets]
Catch some fish
Catch some fish
This is the way we catch some fish
Some fish are good.

Now we put the good fish into baskets
[smile and pretend to put fish into baskets]
Into baskets
Into baskets
Now we put the good fish into baskets
Some fish are good.

Then we throw the bad fish away
[frown and pretend to throw away bad fish]
Bad fish away
Bad fish away
Then we throw the bad fish away
Some fish are good.

Jesus told the story about bad fish and good
[point upward]
Bad fish and good
Bad fish and good
Jesus told the story about bad fish and good
Some fish are good.

Good, Not Bad

I can be good for God *[point to self, then upward to God]*
I don't want to be bad. *[shake head "no"]*
Jesus teaches us to be good. *[point to self, then upward to Jesus]*
When we're good, God is happy, not sad. *[draw a smile on own face with index fingers]*

song/verse

What You Need
• duplicated page

What to Do
1. Learn the song, "Some Good Fish," to sing with the children.
2. Sing the song to the tune of "This is the Way We…."
3. Do the actions with the children.
4. Help children learn as much of the song as they can remember, as the song tells the story in today's lesson.
5. Say the action rhyme, "Good, Not Bad."

•Fish•

coloring

What You Need

- duplicated page for each child
- crayons

What to Do

1. Hold the picture up so that all the children can see it while you read the story out loud to the children.

2. Afterward, while the children color their pictures, talk about things that are good. Say, **We have some favorite foods that are good, like ice cream or celery with peanut butter. We can do good things for other people. We can have a good time with someone we like being with. Good things are all around us. We can be good for God, too. Jesus teaches us to be good.**

• A Good Day •

"**T**here's my boy," Uncle Dave said when he opened the door. "Are you ready to help me today?"

"What are we going to do?" Trevor asked.

Uncle Dave lifted Trevor into the car and fastened the seatbelt on his car seat. "We have lots to do today. Let's get your seat belt on. Wearing a seat belt is GOOD." Uncle Dave said.

Soon, they were at Grandma's house where they raked leaves.

Trevor nodded. "Helping someone is GOOD," he said.

Then they went to the pet store. "I want a new fish for my fish tank," Uncle Dave said. "Can you help me pick out a GOOD fish?"

Trevor pointed at a fish. "I like this purple one," he said.

Uncle Dave said, "That's a GOOD choice."

After they took the fish to Uncle Dave's house, it was time to go home.

"What did you two do today?" Dad asked.

Trevor went to get his pajamas. "Uncle Dave and I did lots of GOOD things today, Dad."

• Caught Being Good Badges •

activity

What You Need

- page duplicated to brightly colored paper, enough to give each child at least one badge during class time
- scissors
- tape

What to Do

1. Before class, cut out several "Caught being good" badges.
2. During class time, stress the concept of being good. Say, **Jesus teaches us to be good.**
3. Each time you see a child being good, fasten a "caught being good badge" to his/her clothing with a loop of tape.

"I was caught being good. Galatians 6:9"

"I was caught being good. Galatians 6:9"

"I was caught being good. Galatians 6:9"

Chapter 6

We Learn to Share

Memory Verse

Do not forget to share with others.
— *Hebrews 13:16*

 ∗Story to Share∗
. . . .

2's and 3's ⤳

Jesus was teaching many people one day. Someone said, "My brother won't share with me."

Jesus said, "You and your brother should both be careful not to be selfish. Jesus told a story about someone who was selfish and would not share.

A farmer harvested much food from his land. The farmer said, "Hmmm. I think I'll build bigger barns to store all my food. Then I won't have to share with anyone. I can keep all this food for myself."

But, God said to the farmer, "You should share with others. Everyone should learn to share what they have."

I's and young 2's ⤳

"My brother will not share with me," someone said to Jesus. Jesus told a story about someone who would not share.

A farmer grew lots and lots of food. But he did not share it with anyone. He wanted to build bigger barns to keep all the food for himself. God said to the farmer, "Everyone should share what they have with others."

Based on Luke 12:16-21

? Questions for Discussion

1. What did the farmer want to do with all his extra food? Build bigger barns and keep it for himself.

2. What does Jesus want us to do with what we have? Share with others.

story visual

What You Need

- page 58 duplicated twice (use tan colored paper if available)
- story poster, page 60
- medium sized paper bag and large paper bag
- tape
- canned and boxed food and a small wrapped treat for each child

What to Do

1. Tape a picture of the barn to a medium sized paper bag. Tape the second picture of the barn to a large paper bag.
2. To tell the story, begin with the medium bag.
3. Show the story poster. Fill the medium bag with food. Then open the bigger bag and put things from the smaller bag in it. End with a bag of treats to share.

• Bigger Barns •

Another Idea

Glue or tape a barn picture onto each of the four sides of a medium-sized box. Set the box in a special place in the classroom. Alert parents ahead of time, asking them to send one canned food item to class with their child. Let children 'fill' the barn with food to share with others.

• Bulletin Board Poster •

Poster Pointer

Story Poster Game: Have children take turns placing a sticker or sticker dot on the poster, like "pin the tail on the donkey" game. Don't use a blindfold, but play the game according to the ages of your toddlers (turn around and try to quickly place a sticker on the poster, or simply take turns putting stickers on until each child has had at least one turn).

bulletin board

What You Need
• pattern on page 60
• glue
• old magazines

What to Do
1. Depending on how you want to use the poster (see ideas below), enlarge, reduce, or simply copy page 60 to fit your bulletin board space.

2. To use the poster as an in-class activity, turn the poster over and use the back side. Provide magazine cutouts of toys, food, and other items toddlers might share with others. Have the children choose some pictures of things they will share with others and glue the pictures onto the back of the poster. Write at top of the picture collage, "I will share."

•Share•

Do not forget to share with others. ~ Hebrews 13:16

• Are You Sharing? Song •

Are You Sharing?

Are you sharing
Are you sharing
With one another
With one another
Jesus teaches us to share our things
Jesus wants us to share our things.
We can share.
We can share.

What You Need
• duplicated page

What to Do
1. Learn the song, "Are You Sharing?"
2. Sing the song with the children, to the tune of "Are You Sleeping?"
3. Say the rhyme, "What Does It Mean to Share?" in a chanting sort of rhythm. Make the rhyme fun by waving arms in the air when saying, "I know, I know."

What Does It Mean to Share?

What does it mean to share?
I know, I know.
Sharing means we let others play with our toys.
That's what sharing means.

What does it mean to share?
I know, I know.
Sharing means we give food to others.
That's what sharing means.

What does it mean to share?
I know, I know.
Sharing means we take time to help.
That's what sharing means.

What does it mean to share?
I know, I know.
Sharing means we tell others about God.
That's what sharing means.

• Share •

easy puzzle

What You Need
- duplicated page for each child
- crayons

What to Do
1. Use this puzzle as a group activity or for one-on-one time with children.
2. Say, **We can find many ways to share. We have many things we can share with others. Let's find some things in our puzzle that we can share with others.**
3. Help the children find and color the following items: fire truck, doll, Bible, cake, jacket, loaf of bread.

• Share •

• Things We Can Share Hidden Pictures •

• Don't Be a Piggy •
Sharing Treat Holder

"DON'T BE A PIGGY."   "SHARE WITH OTHERS."

simple craft

What You Need
- page duplicated to pink or tan paper for each child
- plastic jar with lid, about 4 inches tall or taller, one per child
- tape
- scissors
- crayons
- age-appropriate treat (cereal pieces, soft candies, popcorn)

What to Do
1. Before class, cut the piggy from the pattern page for each child.
2. Say, **Jesus told a story about a selfish farmer who wouldn't share with others. We should remember to share. When we don't share, we are like piggies who don't share. Jesus teaches us to share.**
3. Have children color the piggy picture.

• Share •

What to Do, continued...

4. Help the children tape the piggy picture onto the side of the jar.
5. Fill the jar with treats.
6. Say, **We can use our piggy treat holders to share with others. What else can we share with others?**

coloring

What You Need
- duplicated page for each child
- crayons

What to Do

1. Hold the picture up so that all the children can see it while you read the story out loud to the children.

2. Afterward, while the children color their pictures, talk about sharing. Say, **Ben and Breanna shared with someone who needed help. What can you share with someone? Jesus teaches us to share.**

• **Share** •

• Ben and Breanna Share •

"Good morning everyone," Mrs. Johnson said. "Let's all gather in the story circle."

Ben watched the door for his friend Scott to come to class. Scott was at class every week.

All the kids sat on the story rug to listen to Mrs. Johnson. It was always fun to listen to a Bible story in Sunday school. But, Mrs. Johnson didn't have her Bible on her lap, like she always did.

"I have some bad news about our friend Scott. His family had a fire in their home. We can help Scott's family when they find another home. We can share food and clothes, and even some toys."

After class, Ben and Breanna's Mom came to pick them up from class. "May we help Scott's family?" Ben asked.

"Yes," Mom answered. "We will share with Scott's family."

"I can give Scott some of my toys," Ben said.

A few days later, Ben and Breanna went with Mom and Dad to take some things to Scott's family. Ben carried his favorite truck to give to his friend. Breanna carried a blanket that she and Ben bought with money they received for their birthday.

Ben and Breanna felt good about sharing with their friend.

• Sharing Game •

What to Do, continued...

4. Have children look to see if they have any pairs of the same picture cards that are the same color. They may put their pairs down in front of them.

5. Have children take turns asking the person on their left, "Do you have any 'blue trucks?'" If that person does have the card, he/she must give it to the one who asked. If they do not, then they do not have to share a card. The children only have to share a card if it is the same picture AND color.

6. Then, the person who was asked for a card gets to ask the person on his/her left.

7. Children may lay down pairs of cards that are the same picture AND color.

8. When no one seems able to share a card, switch and have the game go the opposite direction, children ask the person on their right. Then, the person sitting opposite them, etc., in order to get all the cards used up and placed in pairs.

9. Each time a child shares a card, say the memory verse.

game

What You Need
• pages 65 and 66, duplicated to card stock, four copies of each page, two copies one color and two of another color
• scissors

What to Do

1. Before class, duplicate the two pattern pages to card stock, four copies of each. Cut out all the cards.

2. Play the game with two to six children in a group.

3. Mix up the cards and place them face-down on a table or play surface. Have each child choose one card at a time until all the cards are chosen. Children will hold their cards so that no one else can see them.

• Share •

■● Chapter 7 ●■
The Persistent Widow

Memory Verse

keep on praying. – *Ephesians 6:18*

 ❋Story to Share❋

2's and 3's ⤳

Jesus told a story to teach us that we should always pray and not give up.

Jesus said, "There was a judge who didn't obey God or care about helping other people. A woman kept coming to the judge and asking for his help. The judge kept sending the woman away. But, finally, the judge decided he was tired of this woman bothering him. He helped the woman, not because he cared about her, but just to stop her from coming to see him."

Jesus said, "God loves you very much and will answer your prayers, always. God wants you to keep talking to him and telling him what you need. Don't give up. Keep praying, and you will see an answer to your prayers."

I's and young 2's ⤳

A woman needed help from a judge. The judge didn't obey God. The judge didn't care about helping people. The woman kept asking for help. The judge kept saying no.

Finally, one day, the judge helped the woman. "Now she will stop coming and bothering me," the judge said.

Jesus told us this story to teach us that God ALWAYS listens to us. God wants us to pray again and again and again. God loves us.

"Keep on praying," Jesus teaches us.

Based on Luke 18:1-8

❓ Questions for Discussion

I. Why did the woman keep going back to the judge? He kept telling her 'no' he wouldn't help her.

2. Does it bother God when we keep praying? NO. God WANTS us to keep praying.

• Topsy-Turvy Story •

story visual

What You Need
- duplicated page
- empty one-pound coffee can with lid
- tape
- construction paper

What to Do

1. Before class, cut the two story strips from the page. Cover the coffee can with paper. Tape one story strip along the bottom edge of the can. Turn the can upside-down. Tape the second story strip along the other edge of the can.

2. To tell the story, turn the can to show the different pictures.

   Say, **Jesus told us this story to teach us that God always listens to our prayers. God wants us to keep praying again, and again, and again. God loves us.** Say the memory verse with the children.

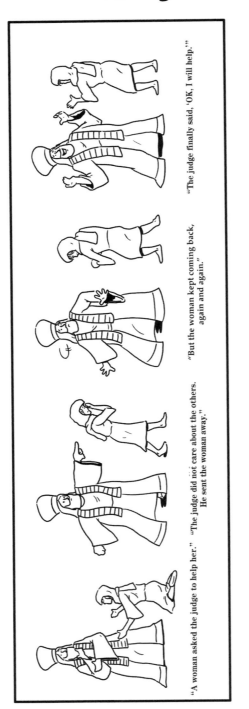

"The judge finally said, 'OK, I will help.'"

"But the woman kept coming back, again and again."

"The judge did not care about the others. He sent the woman away."

"The judge did not care about the others." "The judge did not care about the others."

"A woman asked the judge to help her."

God wants us to keep asking him for what we want and need. Our Bible says, "Keep on praying."

More ideas
Duplicate story strips. Cut out and tape the strips to form a headband for children to wear. Use strips for the bulletin board, room border or as a border for the doors of the room.

• Pray •

• Bulletin Board Poster •

Poster Pointer

Puzzle Match: Duplicate two posters to card stock for each student. Cut one poster into 3 or 4 puzzle pieces. Help children place the puzzle pieces onto the intact poster to assemble the puzzle.

bulletin board

What You Need
- pattern on page 70
- stickers with the image of Jesus
- construction paper or card stock

What to Do
1. Depending on how you want to use the poster (see ideas below), enlarge, reduce, or simply copy page 70 to fit your bulletin board space.

2. To use the poster as an in-class activity, have the children put at least one sticker of Jesus on the poster to help instill the concept that Jesus teaches us things, and also to help them understand to whom they are talking when they pray. Say, **Let's put some stickers of Jesus on our pictures. Jesus teaches us that we should keep praying and not stop. Jesus listens when we pray.**

•Pray•

Keep on Praying.
~ Ephesians 6:18

• We Can Pray •
Room Decoration

bulletin board

What You Need
- page duplicated to brightly colored paper, at least one per child
- scissors
- yarn or fishing line
- tape

What to Do
1. Before class, duplicate several copies of the praying people.
2. Have the children each color a picture of the praying family.
3. Hang the praying family figures from the ceiling with yarn, or fasten to the wall. You may also line the bulletin board with the pictures.
4. Say, **Jesus teaches us to pray. Let's pray together.**

Option
You may enlarge the page and duplicate the enlarged figures for better handling by toddlers.

• Pray •

song/verse

What You Need

• duplicated pages 70 and 72, one for each child.

What to Do

1. Practice singing the song, "Pray to God," to the tune of "Praise Him, Praise Him."

2. Sing the song with the children. Fold your hands when you say the word PRAY.

3. Recite the "Keep on Praying" story verse. Show the children the picture of the judge and the woman from page 70. Stress that Jesus is not like the impatient judge. Jesus wants to hear from us.

4. Encourage the children to take the duplicated pages home to share with their parents.

• Pray •

• Pray Song and Story Verse •

Pray to God

Pray to Him, pray to Him, all you little children
God hears us
God hears us
Pray to Him, pray to Him, all you little children
God hears us
God hears us.

Keep on Praying

Jesus told a story about a woman and a judge.
The woman asked for help each day.
The judge said, "No, just go away."
Finally the judge grew weary.
And said, "Okay, I'll help you. Okay!"

Jesus wants us to know that he's not like that judge.
He listens to our prayers each day.
He'll never tell us to "go away."
Even when it seems a long time.
Jesus answers our prayers in a special way.

• Never Ending •

What You Need
- duplicated page for each student
- round snack cans, any size, with lids
- colorful wrapping paper
- tape
- crayons

What to Do
1. Before class, cover the snack cans with colorful paper.
2. Give each child a covered snack can and the picture strip from the duplicated page.
3. Children may color the pictures if desired.
4. Help the children wrap the picture strip around the snack can. Tape the ends to hold the picture strip onto the can.
5. Have children roll the cans on the floor. Say often, **Jesus wants us to keep praying, just like we are keeping this toy moving.**

Pray to God

Pray to Him, pray to Him,
all you little children
God hears us
God hears us
Pray to Him, pray to Him,
all you little children
God hears us
God hears us.

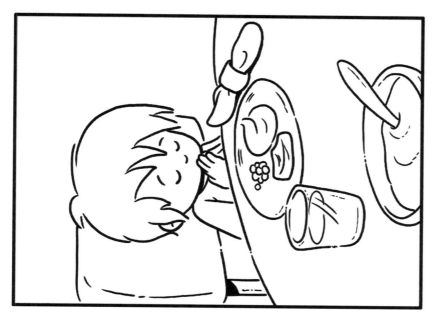

• Pray •

coloring

What You Need
- duplicated page for each child
- crayons

What to Do

1. Hold the picture up so that all the children can see it while you read the story out loud to the children.

2. Afterward, while the children color their pictures, talk about prayer. Say, **Sometimes we pray about something and it seems to take a long time for God to answer our prayer. Jesus teaches us to keep on praying.**

• Keep Praying •

"Daddy didn't get a new job yet," Hannah told Grandma. "Daddy says we should just keep praying."

Grandma hugged Hannah. "Daddy is right," she said. "We should always keep praying until God answers our prayers."

Hannah helped Grandma fold some bath towels. "We have been praying for a long time," Hannah said.

Grandma stopped folding towels and pulled Hannah onto her lap. She opened her Bible and began to read to Hannah. "Jesus told a story about a woman who needed help from a judge. The judge kept sending the woman away. The woman came back again and again. The judge got very tired of listening to the woman. Finally, he gave her what she wanted.

Jesus said we should keep praying. But, he is not like the judge who kept sending the woman away. Jesus cares about us very much. He wants us to keep praying so that we will not worry. When we talk to Jesus, he helps us not to worry."

Grandma started to fold her hands to pray with Hannah. But, the doorbell rang. It was Hannah's Mom and Dad. "Guess what?" Daddy said. "I just got a telephone call. I have a new job!"

Everyone was very happy.

Hannah took Grandma's hand, and Daddy's hand. "Hold hands with us," she said to Mommy. "We should keep on praying. Jesus wants to know even when we are happy about something."

The family prayed together.

• Erasable Slate •

easy puzzle

What You Need
- pages 75 and 76, duplicated for each child
- clear plastic page protectors for 3-hole binder
- cardboard
- crayons
- paper towels
- tape

What to Do
1. Give each child both duplicated pages. Help children put the cardboard between the two pages, with the printing on both pages facing outward.
2. Slip the pages and cardboard inside the clear, plastic page protector.
3. Tape the open end closed.
4. Children may finish both puzzles, then wipe off the crayon with a paper towel.

•Pray•

"Jesus hears our prayers."

Chapter 8

The Prodigal Son

Memory Verse

Return to me and I will return to you.
– Malachi 3:7

Story to Share

2's and 3's →

A son said to his father, "Give me all my share of the family's money." Then, the son went far away. He lived in a way that would not please his father.

Soon, the son's money was all gone. He had nothing to eat. He had no place to live.

He went to a farmer and asked for a job feeding pigs.

Finally, the son said, "If I go back to my father's house, at least I can ask to be a servant."

The son went home. The father saw him and was filled with great joy. He ran to his son and hugged and kissed him.

God is happy when his children return to Him. God wants to welcome us back into his family and make us his special child.

I's and young 2's →

A son took all his money and left home. But, the son did some bad things. When the son had no money left, he asked a farmer for a job feeding pigs. The son went back to his father. The father was very happy to see his son back home. Jesus teaches us that God is happy when we are his children. Jesus teaches us to always be God's child.

Based on Luke 15:11-32

 ## Questions for Discussion

1. When the son was hungry, what did he get a job doing? Feeding pigs.

2. How did the father feel when his son came home? He was very happy.

story visual

What You Need

- duplicated page, two copies
- large juice can, both ends intact
- tape
- scissors
- crayons

What to Do

1. Before class, cut the faces from the two copies of the pattern page. Draw a frown on one face and a smile on the other. Tape one face to each end of the can.

2. When you tell about the Prodigal Son leaving home, roll the visual away from you, to a child.

3. When you tell about the Prodigal Son coming home, have the child roll it back to you.

•Return•

• A Come-back Son •

More Ideas

After you have used the visual to tell the story, let the children take turns rolling the 'come-back son' to each other. Duplicate two copies of the face for each child. Cut out the circles for each child. Glue the face circles together, with a wooden paint stirrer between the pieces, for a handle. Have the children use crayons to make a smile on one face and a frown on the other. Have children hold their happy/sad faces up and turn to the appropriate side while you retell the story. The son was sad when he was away from home. He was happy when he came back into his father's house.

• Bulletin Board Poster •

bulletin board

What You Need
- pattern on page 80
- tape

What to Do
1. Depending on how you want to use the poster (see ideas below), enlarge, reduce, or simply copy page 80 to fit your bulletin board space.
2. To use the poster as an in-class activity, duplicate the poster for each child.
3. Help the children fold the page on the two lines that divide the scenes.
4. Tape the seams together to form a tri-fold picture.
5. Have the children turn the tri-fold picture to the three different scenes while you retell the story.

Poster Pointer

Bulletin Board Learning: Duplicate all eight posters, a different color for each. Fasten all eight posters to a bulletin board. Have a safe stool nearby, so that the children may stand on the stool and touch the posters. Say, **Can you find the blue picture? Touch the blue picture while I tell you the Bible story.**

• Return •

Return to me and I will return to you.
— Malachi 3:7

• Big Happy Puppet •

Return to me and I will return to you.
~Malachi 3:7

Shake Your Puppet

If you're happy to be God's child,
shake your puppet.
If you're happy to be God's child,
shake your puppet.
God says, Return to me
and I'll return to you.
If you're happy to be God's child,
shake your puppet.

simple craft

What You Need
- duplicated page for each child
- gallon plastic milk jug for each child (clean, no lids, labels removed)
- glue
- safety scissors
- crayons

What to Do
1. Before class, cut out the face, song and verse strip from the page.
2. Turn the milk jugs upside-down, so the handles are toward the bottom.
3. Help the children glue the face onto the milk jugs.
4. Glue the verse strip and song strip on the milk jugs.
5. Have the children draw a smile on the face.
6. Say, the memory verse.
7. Sing song to the tune of "If You're Happy and You Know It," having children shake the big happy puppets while they sing.

• Return •

song/verse

What You Need
- duplicated page

What to Do
1. Learn the song and rhyme on this page.
2. Sing, "I'm God's C-H-I-L-D" to the tune of "The B-I-B-L-E."
3. Tell the children, C-H-I-L-D spells child. We are God's children.
4. Say the action verse with the children, showing them the actions.

• I'm God's Child Song •

I'm God's C-H-I-L-D

I'm God's C-H-I-L-D
I'm God's C-H-I-L-D
God says, "I'll return to you, if you'll return to me.
I'm God's C-H-I-L-D.

Action Verse

I am God's child *[point to self, then point to God]*

God loves me. *[hug self]*

God says I'll return to you *[roll arms toward self]*

If you'll return to me. *[roll arms toward God]*

• Return •

• Go and Return Game •

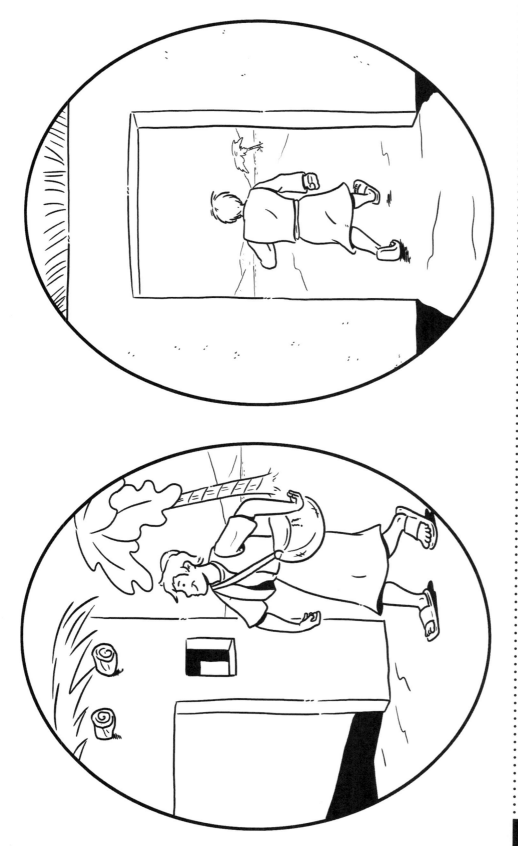

game

What You Need
- poster board
- duplicated page
- scissors
- tape
- CD player with music CD of Sunday school songs

What to Do
1. Before class, cut the two pictures from the page. Glue each picture onto a piece of poster board.
2. Tape the pictures to opposite sides of the floor. Have the children walk, hop or turn in circles from one picture to the other.
3. Say, **The boy left home, but returned to his father. God says, "Return to me and I will return to you."**

• Return •

coloring

What You Need
- duplicated page for each child
- crayons

What to Do
1. Hold up a copy of the picture so all the children can see it as you tell the story.
2. Afterward, while the children color their pictures, say the memory verse with the children.

• Return •

• Levy Comes Back •

"I don't want to watch that movie," Levy said. His sister chose a movie last night. It was his turn.

"We only have this movie for today," Dad said. "We will let you choose tomorrow."

Levy went to his room. "I don't want to be with you," he said to his family.

Levy sat on his bed. He hugged his favorite teddy bear. Then he sat on the floor and played with his trains. He read a book.

Finally, Levy opened the door. He couldn't hear a movie playing. Was his family still downstairs? He tiptoed down the hall and looked into the living room. Mom and Dad were on the couch, talking. Levy's sister was sitting on the chair, reading a book.

Dad saw Levy. "Are you ready to come and join us?" he asked. "We've been waiting for you."

"Did you watch the movie yet?" Levy asked.

"Of course not," Levy's sister said. "It's family time. We can't have family time without YOU."

Dad held out his arms for Levy to come sit on his lap. Mom hugged Levy. Sister hugged Levy.

"We are glad you came back to join us," Dad said.

• Go and Return Maze •

easy puzzle

What You Need
- duplicated page for each child
- crayons

What to Do
1. Give each child a puzzle page.
2. Say, **There are two puzzles on our page. First we must help the boy go away from home. Follow the money to the farm where the pigs are. Now, follow the hearts to help the boy find his way home.**
3. Help younger children follow the two mazes on the page.
4. Say, **God loves us and wants us to be his children. Sometimes we wander away from God by sinning and doing things that do not please God. But, God is always ready to welcome us back into his arms.**

•Return•

• A Boy Comes Home •

simple craft

What You Need
- duplicated page for each child
- empty toilet tissue tube for each child
- scissors
- tape
- 20-inch pieces of yarn
- crayons

What to Do
1. Cut the folding "boy" picture strip and verse box from the page for each child.
2. Have the children color the boy figures.
3. Fold the boy picture strip in half. Tape the strip over the yarn so it will move.
4. Tape the verse box onto the tube.
5. Thread the yarn through the tube. Tie the ends together.
6. Show the children how to pull on the yarn to make the boy disappear into the tube, then appear again.
7. Say, **The boy went away from home, then came back.**

"Return to me and
I will return to you."
~*Malachi 3:7*

• Return •

▪● Chapter 9 ●▪

More Jesus Teaches Me Activities

song

What You Need
• duplicated page

What to Do
1. Learn the song "Jesus Teaches Me." Sing to the tune of "Row, Row, Row Your Boat."
2. You may sing the verse that corresponds with each week's lesson, or sing the entire song when all the lessons have been taught.
3. This is a good activity to send home with the children at the end of the period so that parents can help them review the lesson themes with this easy song.

• Jesus Teaches Me Song •

Jesus Teaches Me

Jesus teaches me
to be a light for Him.
I'm glad Jesus teaches me
To be a light for Him.

Jesus teaches me
to grow strong in the Lord.
I'm glad Jesus teaches me
To grow strong in the Lord.

Jesus teaches me
To obey His Word.
I'm glad Jesus teaches me
To obey His Word.

Jesus teaches me
To forgive my friends.
I'm glad Jesus teaches me
To forgive my friends.

Jesus teaches me
To be good for God.
I'm glad Jesus teaches me
To be good for God.

Jesus teaches me
To share what I have.
I'm glad Jesus teaches me
To share what I have

Jesus teaches me
To keep on praying.
I'm glad Jesus teaches me
To keep on praying.

Jesus teaches me
To always be God's child.
I'm glad Jesus teaches me
To always be God's child.

• Book Cover •

activity

JESUS TEACHES ME.

What You Need
- page reduced in size and duplicated to brightly colored paper
- story posters from lessons 1-8, reduced in size and duplicated to brightly colored paper
- clear, self-stick plastic
- clear, heavy tape, around 2 inches wide

What to Do
1. Duplicate book cover and 8 story posters from this book.
2. Cover both sides of each poster and the book cover with clear self-stick plastic.
3. Use clear, heavy tape to form a binding on the outside of the book, as well as along the seams of each page in the book.
4. Let children hold the books as you review the lessons or memory verses.

•Extras•

activity

What You Need
- pages 90 and 91, duplicated
- items listed under desired idea for using the story shapes

What to Do
Use the easy shapes on pages 90 and 91 with one of the following ideas:

1. **FELT FIGURES** for felt boards.
2. **CRAFT FOAM FIGURES** to play with.
3. **CARD STOCK FIGURES** for puppets with craft stick handles.
4. **MAGNETIC FIGURES** for a magnet board.

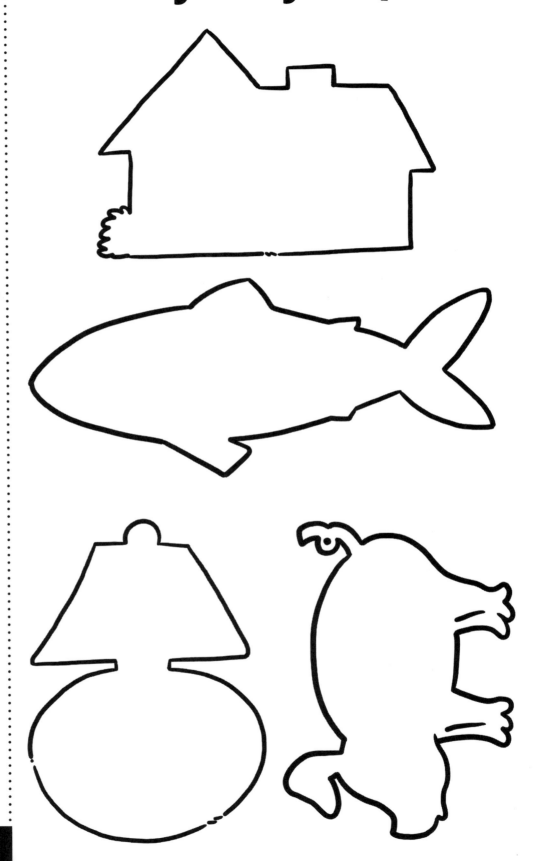

•Extras•

bulletin board

What You Need

- duplicated page, as is, or enlarged
- camera
- tape

What to Do

1. Enlarge the pattern and duplicate.

2. Fasten the poster to a bulletin board or to the wall at children's eye level.

3. Take a photo of each child and print the photos.

4. Fasten the photos to the bulletin board or wall. Say to the children, **Jesus teaches Jacob. Jesus teaches Leann. Jesus teaches Rachel.**

5. Another idea: Tape a poster to your door to greet children.

• Bulletin Board Poster •

JESUS TEACHES ME

• Jesus Teaches Me Lacing Cards •

simple craft

What You Need
- page duplicated to colorful paper for each child
- thin cardboard
- hole punch
- yarn

What to Do
1. Before class, glue the pattern page on a piece of thin cardboard. Use a hole punch to punch holes around the picture.
2. Have children lace the yarn through the holes.
3. Say, **Jesus is teaching the children in the picture. Jesus teaches us many things in God's Word. We are happy to learn from Jesus.**

JESUS TEACHES ME.

easy puzzle

What You Need
- pages 94 and 95, duplicated to card stock
- scissors
- optional – clear, self-stick plastic

What to Do
1. Before class, duplicate and cut out the pieces for at least one puzzle for playtime or for one-on-one time. You may choose to make a puzzle for each child to take home. You may cover the puzzle pieces with clear, self-stick plastic if you wish.

2. Use the puzzle as a review for the lessons and/or memory verses in lessons 1-8. As children are assembling the puzzle, say something about each puzzle piece. For example: **Here is a picture of a lamp. Our memory verse is "Let your light shine."**

• Review Puzzle •

Let's not become weary in doing good.

Do not forget to share with others.

Hear the Word

Forgive from your heart.

Do not forget to share with others.

Return to me and I will return to you.

Let your light shine.

If you love me you will obey.

Let's not become weary in doing good.

Keep on praying.

activity

What You Need
- duplicated page
- craft foam
- glue
- scissors
- empty thread spools, any size
- tempera paints in shallow pans
- plain paper
- paint cover-ups

What to Do
1. Before class, cut the shapes from the pattern page. Trace each shape onto craft foam. Cut the shape from the craft foam. Glue the shape onto one end of an empty thread spool.

2. Put paint cover-ups on the children. Show children how to dip the 'stamp' into the paint, then press the stamp onto paper.

3. Children may make a picture to take home, a card for someone, or stamp the shapes onto strips of paper for a bulletin board.

•Extras•

• Easy Stamping Fun •